Safe   in the   arms   of   night.

Good   night,   gray   mares,

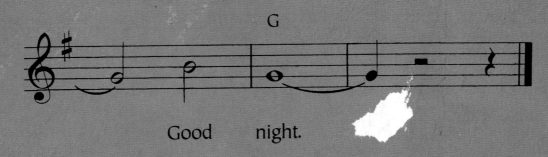

Good   night.

Repeat with each verse.

The Animals' Lullaby

by Tom Paxton

illustrated by

ERICK INGRAHAM

MORROW JUNIOR BOOKS

New York

Acrylics were used for the full-color art.
The text type is 17-point Tiepolo.
Text copyright © 1993 by Tom Paxton
Illustrations copyright © 1993 by Erick Ingraham
Music and words copyright © 1993 by Pax Music, ASCAP

Printed in Singapore at Tien Wah Press.
1   2   3   4   5   6   7   8   9   10
Library of Congress Cataloging-in-Publication Data
Paxton, Tom.
The animals' lullaby / by Tom Paxton ; illustrated by Erick
Ingraham.
p.   cm.
Summary: Animals return home, the sandman arrives, and children
snuggle in their beds at the close of another day.
ISBN 0-688-10468-1.—ISBN 0-688-10469-X (lib. bdg.)
1. Children's songs—United States—Texts.   [1. Animals—Songs
and music.   2. Bedtime—Songs and music.   3. Lullabies.   4. Songs.]
I. Ingraham, Erick, ill.   II. Title.
PZ8.3.P2738Ao   1993
782.42164'0268—dc20   92-18841   CIP   AC

To Midge,
whose idea this was
—T. P.

Gray mares are running
Over the fields in flight,
Home to their stalls to slumber,
Safe in the arms of night.

Good night, gray mares,
Good night.

Swift doves are flying
Back from the cloudy west.
Quickly they race the shadows
Home to their treetop nest.

Good night, doves,
Good night.

Otters come sliding,
Splashing their carefree way,
Playfully heading homeward,
Closing another day.

Good night, otters,
Good night.

Chipmunks are dashing
Over the twigs and cones
Into a nestle-down burrow
Under the mossy stones.

Good night, chipmunks,
Good night.

White swans are gliding,
Feathers as soft as snow.
Gently they lead their young ones
Back where the rushes grow.

Good night, swans,
Good night.

Shy deer are standing
Under the tall, dark pines.
Flickering beams of sunset
Glow through the hanging vines.

Good night, deer,
Good night.

Bright fish are swimming
Down through a coral sea.
Deep in the clear blue water,
Day is a memory.

Good night, fish,
Good night.

Porcupines cuddle,
Slowly making their beds,
Huddling there together,
Nodding their prickly heads.

Good night, porcupines,
Good night.

Foxes are drowsy
Deep in their cool, dark den.
Sleep, little red-tailed foxes,
Morning will come again.

Good night, foxes,
Good night.

Squirrels are sighing
Under their bushy tails,
High in the hickory branches,
Safe from the howling gales.

Good night, squirrels,
Good night.

Puppies are squirming
Close by their mama's side.
Tired from all their romping,
Off to their dreams they ride.

Good night, puppies,
Good night.

Kittens are mewing,
Slowly licking their paws,
Washing their little faces,
Yawning their little jaws.

Good night, kittens,
Good night.

Red sun is setting—
Colors across the sky.
Evening is slowly falling,
Sandman is coming by.

Good night, sun,
Good night.

Children are snuggling,
Warm in their patch-quilt beds.
Their sleepy eyes are closing;
Lullabies dance through their heads.

Good night, children,

Good night.

THE ANIMALS' LULLABY

Gray   mares   are   run- ning

Ov-   er   the   fields   in   flight,

Home   to their   stalls   to   slum- ber,